101 Coolest Things to Do in France

Introduction

So you're going to France, huh? You lucky lucky thing! You are sure in for a treat because France is, without a doubt, one of the most special travel destinations on the face of the planet. It offers something for every visitor, so whether you are into eating yourself silly, strolling the aisles of world renowned galleries, or lazy beach days.

This guide will take you on a journey from the major cities like Paris, Marseilles, Lyon, and Nice, through to places in the hills, countryside, and beaches like Chartres, Corsica, and the Loire Valley.

In this guide, we'll be giving you the low down on:
- the very best things to shove in your pie hole, whether you need to hunt out the best

French eclairs, or you want to dine in Michelin star restaurants

- incredible festivals, from electronic beach festivals through to an open-air opera festival set within a Roman theatre
- the coolest historical and cultural sights that you simply cannot afford to miss like world class art museums, and some of the globe's most celebrated churches and cathedrals
- the most incredible outdoor adventures, whether you want to bungee jump off a bridge in the south of France, or you fancy having a snorkelling adventure in Corsica
- where to shop for authentic souvenirs so that you can remember your trip to France forever
- the places where you can party like a local and make new friends
- and tonnes more coolness besides!

Let's not waste any more time — here are the 101 coolest things not to miss in France!

1. Take a Romantic Boat Ride on Canal St Martin

The River Seine is, without a doubt, the most famous waterway in Paris, but it is certainly not the only one, and we happen to think that the Canal St Martin is even more charming. The canal was ordered by Napoleon in 1802 as a way to transport fresh water to locals so they wouldn't get sick, but these days it primarily has an ornamental use, and we think there's nothing quite as romantic as taking a boat ride on this stretch of water.

(Canal Saint-Martin, Paris)

2. Tuck into the Rosette Sausages of Lyon

For meat lovers on a trip to France, there is much more than hulks of steak with peppercorn sauce, and we love to explore the nooks and crannies of the country to eat delicious regional treats. The Rosette sausages of Lyon are something extra special, in our opinion. This simple sausage is made from pork leg, garlic, salt, and peppercorns, and we think it's best eaten just as it is on an antipasti platter.

3. Take in a Ballet at Palais Garnier

As you stroll the streets of Paris, it's easy to imagine yourself immersed in the pages of a fairytale, and one way to extend the magic is by taking in a show at the Palais Garnier, a theatre that opened in 1875 as a place to stage operas in the city. These days, you are more likely to catch a ballet performance there, and with its capacity to seat 1900 people, we think that it's one of the grandest and most spectacular arts destinations in Europe.

(8 Rue Scribe, Paris; www.operadeparis.fr/en)

4. Visit the World's Largest Museum, The Louvre

France is such a haven for arts lovers that it would be possible for us to write 101 coolest galleries in the country, let alone all of the other things to do. But in the name of variety, we have had ourselves back, but a guide to France really wouldn't be complete without mentioning The Louvre, which might just be the most famous art gallery in the world. In fact, it is the world's largest museum, containing 35,000 objects from prehistory and up to the present day. From Egyptian Antiquities to Islamic Art to Renaissance decorative objects, The Louvre needs a day of your time at the very least.

(75001, Paris; www.louvre.fr)

5. Catch a Show at the Festival d'Avignon

If you love nothing more than to spend your free time going to the theatre, you need to know about the annual Avignon Festival, which is one of the most acclaimed performing arts festivals on the face of the planet. Over 40 productions are put on across the month of July, across venues large and small. So whether you want to see a reboot of a Shakespeare classic or a dynamic piece of contemporary dance, there will be something to suit your theatrical tastes at the festival. *(www.festival-avignon.com/en)*

6. Find Something Special at La Braderie de Strasbourg

If you're a bargain hunter at heart, you would do well to avoid the pricey boutique stores that line the streets of Paris, and instead to find your way to La Braderie de Strasbourg, which is one of the most epic flea markets anywhere in France. This market takes over Strasbourg on the last weekend of July, and over 400 sellers come to show their wares, comprising artwork, antique furniture, awesome vintage clothing, and lots more besides.

7. Catch a Movie at Le Louxor

Paris is the kind of city that bears endless exploration. But when you can't face another gallery and you simply want to relax, we have just the ticket for you: Le Louxor Cinema. This cinema is a part of local history, and it opened way back in 1921 when it was the place to watch silent movies. It closed during World War II, and became a drug den and then gay disco, but reopened triumphantly in 2013. As well as showing wonderful movies, it can also claim to have the greatest cinema bar in the city.

(170 Boulevard de Magenta, Paris;
www.cinemalouxor.fr)

8. Ascend Europe's Largest Sand Dune, Dune du Pilat

When you think of places in Europe to frolic in the sand, France might not be the first country that springs to mind, but little did you know that, in fact, the largest sand dune in the continent can be found in France. This dune is almost 3 kilometres long and has a height of 110 metres. It's possible to climb all the way to the top of the soft sand and then roll all the way back down. Or if you feel like something more exhilarating, you can body board down at a high speed.

(www.dune-pyla.com/en)

9. Pick a Bottle From a Historic Wine Cellar in Paris

Let's face it, a wine lover is never going to be disappointed on a trip to France. But if you don't have the time to drive out into the wine country, there are still some great places in Paris where you can pick up a bottle (or five). It's not easy to narrow it down to one favourite spot, but if we had to choose it's Les Caves Auges, a wine cellar that's been open since 1850, and where Proust used to stock up his cellar. Top tip: they have a tasting day every Saturday.

(116 Boulevard Haussmann, Paris; www.cavesauge.com)

10. Enjoy the Beauty of Parc de le Tete d'Or

One of the loveliest thing about visiting French cities is that although they are filled with a cosmopolitan atmosphere, they are also very green, and Lyon is perhaps the greenest of all the French cities. In fact, the Parc de Tete d'Or is the largest urban park in the whole country, covering an area of 117 hectares. In the park, you'll find a zoo, a boules court, horse riding, mini golf, and many other attractions.

(www.lyon.fr/lieu/lieux-danimation/parc-de-la-tete-dor.html)

11. Sample Some French Fare at Bastille Market in Paris

There's no doubt that Paris is one of the most magnificent food cities on the face of the earth, but there is more to the local food culture than fancy restaurants. If you want to eat somewhere that's more alive, not to mention kinder to the wallet, the open air Bastille Market is a must visit. This is the place where local chefs come to purchase their produce so you know it's good. We can think of nothing better than grabbing some stinky cheese, crusty bread, and sour olives from the market and heading to the riverbank to eat them.

(13 Boulevard Beaumarchais, Paris)

12. Have a Snorkelling Adventure Off Corsica's Coast

When you think of beautiful islands around Europe, you might think of Greek islands like Crete or the islands of Italy like Sardinia. Well, France has its fair share of paradise islands too, and it doesn't get much more beautiful than Corsica. There are breath taking white sandy beaches on Corsica, but also clear waters to explore. If you feel like having an adventure, snorkelling in the waters of Corsica is a fantastic idea. In the waters you'll find bream, starfish, congers, moray eels, barracuda, and more.

13. Discover the Cave Paintings of Grotte de Font de Gaume

If you can tear yourself away from the fromageries and patisseries dotted around France for a hot second, there are also some wonderful historic attractions to be found, and we are talking more than churches and castles. In the Grotte de Font de Gaume, you can look at some of the most incredible prehistoric cave paintings to be found anywhere in Europe. There's more than two hundred painted or engraved representations of bison, horses, mammoths, reindeer, and more.

(1-4 Avenue des Grottes, 24620 Les Eyzies-de-Tayac-Sireuil; http://font-de-gaume.monuments-nationaux.fr)

14. Learn About the History of Paris at Carnavalet Museum

If you are a history buff, there is plenty to be explored right across France, and the Carnavalet Museum acts as the local history museum for Paris. The setting of the museum itself, located across two 16th and 17th mansions, is stunning in itself, and the collection is just as impressive. Inside, you'll find medieval and Gallo-Roman artefacts, items from the French revolution, sculptures, furniture, paintings, and lots more besides. *(23 Rue de Sévigné, Paris; www.carnavalet.paris.fr)*

15. Get Decadent With Macarons From Pierre Herme

If you have a sweet tooth, Paris is a city that is not going to disappoint. As you hop from bakery to bakery, be sure not to miss out on the decadent macarons that can be found across the city, and indeed across the country. There is nobody who can make pastries quite like the French God of Sweets, Pierre Herme, and a trip to one of his bakeries is a must. The macarons are light and perfectly balanced, and it's more than possible to eat a whole box. *(89 Boulevard Malesherbes, 75008 Paris; www.pierreherme.com)*

16. Visit a Stunning Royal Chateau, Palace of Fontainebleau

Not everyone is in the position to be able to enjoy a complete trip of France, but even if you only make it to Paris (and let's face it, that really wouldn't be so bad) there are still some easy day trips that you can make to explore outside of the city a little. One of the best of these is a trip to the Palace of Fontainebleau.

This is one of the largest French royal chateaux, located just around 55 kilometres southeast of Paris. This chateau dates all the way back to the 13th century, and we are particularly enamoured by its French renaissance gardens.

(www.musee-chateau-fontainebleau.fr)

17. Discover a World of Classic Automobiles at Cite de l'Automobile

If classic cars do it for you, you cannot leave France before you visit the Cite de l'Automobile, a classic car museum that has the largest displayed collection of automobiles in the world, and it specifically has the largest and most comprehensive Bugatti collection. The cars are stunning simply to look at, but the free audio guide will give you a much better idea of the importance of each car in automobile history.

(15 Rue de l'Épée, 68100 Mulhouse; www.citedelautomobile.com/ en)

18. Dance, Dance, Dance at Vieilles Charrues Festival

When you think of countries around the world that are famous for their summer festivals, it is unlikely that France would be the first country that springs to mind. But believe it or not, the French totally know how to throw a party, and if you're planning a trip to France during the summer months, you need to etch Vieilles Charrues into your itinerary. It is hosted every July in the Brittany region, and previous performers have included Muse, Portishead, and Bruce Springsteen.

(www.vieillescharrues.asso.fr)

19. Dine on Le Calife, a 5 Star Cruising Restaurant

There's no shortage of phenomenal restaurants to be found along the streets of Paris, but if you fancy a dining experience with a bit of a difference, Le Calife is something you should know about. This is a floating restaurant that cruises the famous River Seine. But this restaurant is not such a success because of this gimmick, but because the food is truly second to none. If you have the opportunity to order the gingerbread ice cream, do not let it pass you by.

(3 Quai Malaquais, Paris; www.calife.com)

20. Climb the Tower of Bordeaux Cathedral

Bordeaux Cathedral is a testament to French architecture, and to say that it's a masterpiece and a labour of love would be an understatement. The construction of the church began in the 12th century, but it wasn't completed until the 16th century, which means that it took 400 years to complete. Because it took so long, you can see that the walls have mismatching colours. If you're feeling adventurous, take the steep climb up the cathedral's tower, where you can view from the city from a vantage point of 50 metres above the ground.

(Place Pey Berland, Bordeaux; http://cathedrale-bordeaux.fr)

21. Indulge in Traditional Crepes at Creperie Au Pressoir

When you visit France, there are plenty of opportunities to be indulgent. The wine! The cheese! The pastries! And let's not forget the delicious crepes. We could eat them for breakfast, lunch, dinner, and snacks in

between, and there is no better place for a
crepe than at Creperie Au Pressoir in a quaint
little village in Carnac in the Brittany region.
They also serve cider, which goes down rather
well too.

(Le Ménec, 56340 Carnac; www.creperie-au-pressoir-carnac.fr)

22. Feel the Grandeur of the Luxembourg Gardens

Paris is a phenomenally attractive city, but
even so, there are times when you might want
to escape the streets and the honking of horns
and to find something a little greener within
Paris. That's when you take yourself to the
Jardin du Luxembourg. Napoleon dedicated
the 23 hectares of the garden to the children
of Paris, and with its puppet shows, boat
rides, and vintage carousels, it's still a place

where you can relax, have fun, and enjoy some fresh air in the city.
(www.senat.fr/visite/jardin/index.html)

23. Tour the Magical Mont-Saint-Michel Island

If you would like to have an adventure away from the mainland on your trip to France, we cannot recommend a visit to the Mont-Saint-Michel island enough. While this island will certainly appeal to history buffs, it's beautiful enough for anyone to enjoy a trip there. This is a medieval settlement off the coast of lower Normandy that is best known for playing host to the Norman Benedictine Abbey of St Michel. Be sure to eat the specialty of the island, omelettes, while you're there too. Here they are whipped vigorously so they are extremely light.

(http://en.normandie-tourisme.fr/discover/normandy-must-sees/the-10-top-normandy-must-sees/mont-saint-michel-106-2.html)

24. Sip on Bubbly at the Maisons of Champagne

Nothing screams elegance and the high life like a delicious glass of champagne. And where does champagne come from? France, of course! And more specifically, an actual place called Champagne that exists a little outside of Paris. When visiting, you have to go to the Maisons de Champagne, which are the houses that produce all of that deliciousness and decadence. Some of the most celebrated names in champagne are Bolinger, Pommery, and Taittinger.

25. Stroll the Gorgeous Gardens of Chateau de Villandry

France is one of those places that has it all. If you love culture, you can stroll around galleries for weeks on end, and if you can't get enough of the outdoors, there are plenty of majestic gardens for you to explore. One of the most celebrated of these is the Chateau de Villandry. The famous Renaissance style gardens there include a water garden, ornamental gardens, and even vegetable gardens.

(Loire-Anjou-Touraine Natural Regional Park, 3 Rue Principale, 37510 Villandry; www.chateauvillandry.fr)

26. Feel the Pulse of Local Life at Cours Saleya Market in Nice

Nice is the perfect place for a relaxing city break within the French Riviera, and when we're in Nice, you can find us at the Cours Saleya market on pretty much every single day of the week. The really great thing about Cours Saleya is that it actually hosts four different markets, so there is something for everyone. There is a beautifully colourful flower market that runs from Tuesday to Sunday, an area dedicated to local fruits and veggies, on Monday there is an antiques market, and you can find a craft market in the evening time.

(www.nicetourisme.com/nice/1396-marche-aux-fleurs-cours-saleya)

27. Keep the Whole Family Entertained at Parc Asterix

For culture vultures, France cannot be beaten, and so you might think that the kids would be somewhat left out on a holiday to France. But with incredible attractions like Parc Asterix, this really doesn't have to be the case at all. Parc Asterix is mostly known for its thrilling rollercoasters and rides, and there is plenty to choose from inside the park. There is even a bobsled rollercoaster that reaches speeds of 80km/hour.

(Oise - Pays de France Natural Regional Park, 60128 Plailly; www.parcasterix.fr)

28. Party at a Trendy Canne Hotspot, Le Baoli

Canne has earned a reputation over the years as the place where the jetset come to socialise and be seen. If you want a taste of French glamour, there is no other place that's quite like it, and a trip to Canne would certainly not be complete without partying in the lap of luxury with the locals. For this, we recommend a jaunt to Le Baoli, a bar-club with comfortable sofas, premium drinks, and a veranda that looks out on to a garden full of palm trees.

(Port Pierre Canto, Boulevard de la Croisette, 06400 Cannes; https://baolicannes.com)

29. Indulge a Cheese Lover at Fromagerie Laurent Dubois

If the idea of gorging on stinky cheese from morning until night is enough to send you to Seventh Heaven, you might decide to never leave France. And who could blame you? Of course, there are plenty of wonderful cheese producers and cheese shops, and perhaps our favourite in Paris is the Fromagerie Laurent Dubois. The selection is out of this world, the staff are incredibly knowledgeable, and the cheese are arranged from mild to strong to help you choose.

(47 Ter Boulevard Saint-Germain, Paris; www.fromageslaurentdubois.fr/fr)

30. Be Transported to Medieval France at Carcassonne

One of the really incredible things about France is that you don't have to contain yourself to museums to get a feeling for the country's incredibly rich history, because historic buildings and ruins can be found everywhere. Carcassonne is a place that history buffs will go crazy for. This is a hilltop town in the south of the country, which is famous for its Cite de Carcassonne, a medieval fortress that dates back for centuries and centuries, and the walls were restored in 1853.

(http://whc.unesco.org/en/list/345)

31. Catch a Live Performance at La Dynamo in Toulouse

Toulouse is a place in France that is all too often overlooked, and yet it is hugely popular with many expats who have moved there, and the tourists who make it to that part of France. It's renowned for its rugby and violets, but there's also a lot of fun to be had. When you want to have a great Friday night out, La Dynamo is the place to catch an awesome show. On one night you'll find French indie bands, the next a spoken word night, and lots more besides.

(Rue Amélie, 31000 Toulouse; www.ladynamo-toulouse.com)

32. Explore the Hidden Bays of Calanques

If you find yourself in Marseilles but would like to explore a little outside of the city, the Parc National des Calenques is just begging to be visited. This is a 20 kilometre stretch of dramatic cliffs that give way to gorgeous turquoise waters. There are two ways of exploring. You can walk along the cliffs, and there are some paths that lead down to the sea. Or you can access the undulating bays by taking a kayak tour from Marseilles.

33. Enjoy Open-Air Opera at Choregies d'Orange

Dating all the way back to 1869, Choregies d'Orange is the oldest festival in all of France, and this is one for high culture lovers because each year it celebrates the very best of French opera performance. What we love most about this festival is that all of the performances take place in a preserved Roman theatre that still has its original stage walls and can seat over 8000 people. All the greatest names in opera have performed at this festival, and it's just as exciting every summer.

(www.choregies.fr)

34. Brush Up Your French Conversation Skills

Something that you'll notice when you're in France is that not everyone will want to speak English with you, or will be able to speak English with you. This means that to have the very best time in France it can be a great idea to brush up on the little bit of French that you learned at school so that you can actually understand some of what's being said to you. There are French language schools dotted all around the country, but we love Coeur de France Ecole de Langues, which is located in the heart of the gorgeous Loire Valley.

(1 Place de la Panneterie, 18300 Sancerre; www.coeurdefrance.com)

35. Ride Through Pine Forests on the Train des Pignes

France is actually a rather large country, and if you are doing a tour of different places, you'll have to think about how you'll get from A to B. For us, there is just no better way to see the country than by train, and there are numerous beautiful train trips. One of the loveliest is Train des Pignes, which runs through Provence from Nice to Digne-les-bains and rises to 1000 metres in height. Taking you from a seaside town to olive groves to snowy mountains, this is a ride not to be missed.

36. Enjoy the Festivities of Lyon's Festival of Lights

Lyon is a place to visit for a whole suite of reasons. It was the birthplace of cinema, it has an incredible cultural scene, historic sights, and terrific gastronomy. This means that Lyon is worth visiting at any time of year, but it's particularly during the Festival of Lights, which is hosted each year at the beginning of December. The festival dates to 1643 when the city was affected by the plague, and local councillors promised to pay tribute to Mary if the town was spared. The festival has now grown and grown into a huge light spectacular.

(www.fetedeslumieres.lyon.fr/en/page/history)

37. Learn Something New at Musee de l'Homme

Paris is a museum city through and through, but the museum culture is very weighted towards the fine arts. If you fancy a different kind of experience, the Musee de l'Homme, an anthropology museum, is definitely worth a visit on a drizzly Paris day. The rather ambitious aim of the museum is to gather everything that defines the human being under one roof. This is where Picasso used to come to look at African art and carvings, so you'll be in good company as a visitor.

(17 Place du Trocadéro et du 11 Novembre, Paris; www.museedelhomme.fr)

38. Party Hard on a Marseilles Rooftop

Although Marseilles is the second most populated city in France, it is all too often overlooked by tourists. This is very much a student city, and that makes it one of the best places in the country to party the night away. There are many bars and clubs to choose from, and one of the best loved amongst locals is called La Friche. This is actually a cultural centre that used to be a tobacco factory, and it's beloved because of it's incredible rooftop bar with stunning views across the city and ocean.

(41 Rue Jobin, 13003 Marseille;
www.lafriche.org/fr)

39. Indulge an Arts Lover at the Nuits de Fourviere Festival

Paris is such a cultural centre of the world that some of the other cities in France can get overlooked, but Lyon is also a wonderful place for cultural events in the country, and one of the most exciting of these is the Nuits de Fourviere Festival, which is a celebration of theatre, music, dance, opera, circus, and cinema that has been running since 1946. Les Nuits gathers every summer and attracts around 130,000 spectators, and it's a must for all arts lovers in France.

(www.nuitsdefourviere.com/en)

40. Drive the Alsace Wine Route

Let's face it. If you are a wine lover, you need to be in France asap. And it's more than possible to spend an entire holiday in France exploring the glorious wines. One of the most magnificent wine producing regions is Alsace, which has been an incredible place for wine production for a thousand years. The wine route here stretches for 170 kilometres, which means there is plenty to explore, and the best way of doing so is by renting a car and taking in the gorgeous French countryside.

41. Enjoy the Fun of the Funfair Museum

Paris is certainly one of the world's greatest cities when it comes to museums, but there is more to see than the grand and celebrated art galleries. If you fancy something a little more light hearted to brighten your day on a drizzly Paris morning, the Musee de Arts Forains, or The Funfair Museum, is the place to be. The museum contains a collection of objects, attractions, and rides dating from 1850-1950. You're also allowed to ride the attractions and play vintage funfair games, so this is a wonderful place to keep kids happy.

(53 Avenue des Terroirs de France, Paris; www.arts-forains.com)

42. Say Hi to the Animals at Zoo de la Fleche

If you are travelling with kids it can be a great idea to spend a day at the zoo so that they have the opportunity to get up close to all kinds of magnificent animals. One of the loveliest zoos is Zoo de la Fleche, and one of the really cool things about this particular zoo is that they have gorgeous wooden cabins where you can stay overnight, among the company of the grizzly bears, arctic wolves, wild tigers, and many other stunning animals.

(Le Tertre Rouge, 72200 La Flèche; www.zoo-la-fleche.com)

43. Learn About Alsace Culture at Musee Alsacien

Unless you are a wine buff obsessed with the various wine producing regions of France, you might not be all that familiar with the Alsation region of France, which can be found towards the east of the country and borders Germany. In Strasbourg, you will find the Musee Alsacien, which can give you a much better idea about the history of this fascinating region, including the lives of Alsation Jews who have lived in the area since the mid 12th century.

(23-25 Quai Saint-Nicolas, 67000 Strasbourg; www.musees.strasbourg.eu)

44. Be Stunned by the Stained Glass of Chartres Cathedral

There is no doubt that France has an incredible array of religious architecture. If this is your particular point of interest you might even feel overwhelmed by the amount of choice, but trust us when we tell you to visit Chartres and the incredible Chartres Cathedral. It can be visited as a day trip from Paris, and it's well worth the effort. It is considered the high point of French Gothic art, with its gorgeous spires and sculptures that cover the church façade.

(16 Cloître Notre Dame, 28000 Chartres; www.cathedrale-chartres.org)

45. Indulge a Cinephile at Institut Lumiere

If you are a total movie buff, something that you may or may not be aware of is that

France, and Lyon specifically, is an incredibly important place when it comes to cinema. This is because the Lumiere brothers lived in Lyon, and they invented the Cinematograph, a motion film camera and projector, which they invented back in the 1890s. Institut Lumiere is found within the house of the famous brothers, and it's a place where you can learn about the brothers, their work, and Lyon's place in cinema history.

(25 Rue du Premier Film, 69008 Lyon; www.institut-lumiere.org)

46. Sip on Beers at a Parisian Microbrewery, Le Triangle

France is very much thought of as a wine drinking nation, but if you are more of a beer drinker, you are far from left out in the cold, and one of our favourite spots to down a delicious glass of beer (or five) is at a Parisian microbrewery called Le Triangle. The house made brews are really special, the prices are really quite good for Paris, and they even have comforting home cooked food as well.

(13 Rue Jacques Louvel-Tessier, 75010 Paris; www.triangleparis.com)

47. Take in the Spectacular Detail of Reims Cathedral

To outsiders, Reims Cathedral might not be one of the most famous buildings in France, but in our opinion it is truly one of the most spectacular religious buildings in the country, and it is, in fact, the place where as many as 34 French sovereigns started their reign in France. The exterior of the building is absolutely laden with statues and statuettes, which makes it an incredible feast of details for even those with no religious inclination.

(Place du Cardinal Luçon, 51100 Reims;
www.cathedrale-reims.com)

48. Tuck into Andouillette Sausages at Troyes

When you think of French food, you might think of heavy cream sauces and crepes, but actually there's an incredible regional variety to French cooking, with many dishes that people outside of France will never have heard about. If you're a meat lover, we think that you'll be just as enamoured by the Andouillette sausages of Troyes as we are. The primary ingredient is pork intestine, but don't let that put you off – they're totally delicious.

49. Have a Ski Adventure at Chamonix-Mont-Blanc

France and Europe generally is typically a spot to explore in the summertime, when there are more daylight hours and when the sun shines down and illuminates the quaint towns and cities in a very special way indeed. But we think that France in the winter should not be discounted, particularly if you're a fan of skiing. Chamonix is one of the oldest ski resorts in the Alps with enduring popularity. If you would prefer to visit in the summer months, it's also a wonderful summer hiking destination.

50. Enjoy the World's Best Croissants at Ble Sucre

There is no better way to start a morning in France than with the flaky and buttery layers of a handmade croissant. Patisseries up and down the country sell incredible croissants, but if we had to pick one place to eat croissants for the rest of our days, that place would be Ble Sucre in Paris. This looks like an everyday place and the prices are very reasonable, but the owner worked as a pastry chef in a three Michelin star restaurant and the quality is second to none.

(7 Rue Antoine Vollon, Paris)

51. Tour a Perfume Factory at Maison Galimard

Grasse, a quaint town in the hills of the French Riviera, is the world centre of perfumes. It is the ideal place to visit if you'd like to purchase some special gifts, and of course, purchase a little something for yourself at the same time. Maison Galimard is a perfume house that dates all the way back to the late 18th century, and they offer free guided tours every day of the year. You'll discover how scents are extracted, blended, and packaged up into delightful perfume bottles.

(73 Route de Cannes, Grasse; www.galimard.com)

52. Take Your Golf Clubs to Golf Du Luberon

If your idea of the perfect relaxing vacation is to hit a few golf balls in a picturesque setting, you have many world class golf courses to choose from while in France. Located in the Alps region, this course is gorgeous with its greenness to say the least. It might not be the best place for novices, but if you can navigate your way around a golf course, Golf Du Luberon will certainly not disappoint.

(Chemin du golf, 04860 Pierrevert; www.golfduluberon.com)

53. Indulge at a Restaurant With 3 Michelin Stars

For the uninitiated in French cuisine, it might seem like Paris is the be all and end all of French gastronomy, but this is far from the case. For an exquisite dining experience with a difference, we recommend finding your way Chagny in the East of France, where a 3 Michelin star restaurant, Maison Lameloise is located. The food here is classic and delicious. Think scallops and Jerusalem artichokes, and apple tart with Granny Smith sorbet for dessert.

(36 Place d'Armes, 71150 Chagny; www.lameloise.fr/en/restaurant-lameloise)

54. Watch a Rugby Match at Toulouse's Stadium

France is very much thought of as a cultural and culinary destination, but what if you love sports? Well, you aren't left out either because this is a country that loves a spot of rugby. If you do have the opportunity, be sure to catch a Rugby match at the Stade Toulousain, the local stadium in Toulouse. This stadium has been used for numerous important matches, including the Rugby World Cup in 2007. There is capacity to seat 19,500, and when full the atmosphere in the stadium is electric. *(114 Rue des Troenes, 31200 Toulouse; www.stadetoulousain.fr)*

55. Chow Down on Lyonnaise Doughnuts, Bugnes

There are many gorgeous sweet treats to be devoured on a trip to France, and each place has its own local specialty. Lyon is a particularly wonderful spot to indulge a sweet tooth, and we can't get enough of the local doughnuts, which go by the name of bugnes.

These are very simple little flat doughnuts made with a thin batter. It's possible to find them flavoured with orange blossom which we find particularly scrumptious.

56. Stroll the Cliffs of Etretat

For a coastal walk that will surely take your breath away, we absolutely adore the white cliffs of Etretat in the northern region of Normandy. These pure white cliffs tower high over the Atlantic Ocean, and provide huge amounts of inspiration for painters such as Monet. There's also a very charming white pebble beach below the cliffs if you fancy catching a few rays.

57. Visit the Largest Science Museum in Europe

France is definitely better known for its commitment to the art world rather than the sciences, but believe it or not, Paris is the home of Europe's largest science museum, Cité des Sciences et de l'Industrie. We think that this is one of the best spots in the city for keeping kids entertained, and there are many incredible things to do and see inside. There's a planetarium where you can gaze at the stars, a submarine to explore, an aquarium, and loads more fun stuff.

(30 Avenue Corentin Cariou, Paris; www.cite-sciences.fr/en/home)

58. Bungee From Pont Napoleon

If you can make it to the south-west of France, where the country borders Spain, we highly recommend doing so. This part of the country has a very different feel, with rustic Basque dishes, and incredible countryside.

One of the ways you might want to immerse yourself in the nature of the region is with a thrilling bungee jump. The place to experience this is a bridge called Pont Napoleon. It was built in 1863, has a height of 63 metres, and is the ultimate spot for thrill seekers in France.

59. Climb the Towers of Notre Dame Cathedral

When it comes to religious architecture, France is one of the most renowned destinations in the world, and even if you aren't especially interested in churches we still think you'll be blown away by the magnificent French Gothic architecture of the Notre-Dame de Paris. This church is a true piece of French history since it was completed way back in the 14th century. The most famous part of the building are the stone gargoyles placed on the outside of the structure. It's also possible to climb the interior towers for a stellar view.

(6 Parvis Notre-Dame - Pl. Jean-Paul II, Paris; www.notredamedeparis.fr)

60. Dance to Live Bands at Main Square Festival

Although Main Square Festival is one of the newer additions to the country's festival scene, Main Square Festival has been steadily growing in popularity simply because the organisers have managed to secure such incredible musical talent year after year. This festival is more targeted towards rockers who enjoy live music than to people who want to dance to electronica, with acts like Muse, Coldplay, Metallica, and Placebo taking to the stage.

(https://mainsquarefestival.fr)

61. Explore Marine Life at Aquarium de la Rochelle

There is more to France than yummy pastries and glasses of wine (although those things are rather delightful), and if you find yourself in the Rochelle region with kids, one of the loveliest things that you can do is head to the Aquarium de la Rochelle, which plays host to 12,000 animals of 600 different species. There are different tanks that represent oceans all over the world, and we always love to see the corals of the Great Barrier Reef.

(Quai Louis Prunier, 17000 La Rochelle; www.aquarium-larochelle.com)

62. Cool Down With Ice Creams From Raimo in Paris

We're gonna level with you; the weather in Paris isn't always that reliable. But if you do happen to find yourself in the French capital on a warm and sunny day, the very best way of cooling down is with a decadent ice cream. And the number one spot for ice cream in the city simply has to be Raimo. This traditional ice cream parlour has the perfect blend of traditional and inventive flavours. The praline flavour goes down a treat on any day of the week, and we go for the orange flower flavour when we want a taste of the exotic.

(59-61 Boulevard de Reuilly, 75012 Paris; www.raimo.fr)

63. Feel the Creativity of Paris at the Paris Autumn Festival

With its gorgeous old opera houses and galleries that showcase work from the past centuries, it can be easy to think of Paris as a city that's stuck in the past, but you'll discover that this is far from the case if you make it to the French capital for the Paris Autumn Festival, a multidisciplinary arts festival that showcases how creative the city really is. You can expect a mix of theatre, dance, film, and visual arts across over 40 venues in the capital. *(www.festival-automne.com)*

64. Hike the Breadth of Corsica on the GR20 Trail

Yes, France is the land of historic buildings and gorgeous stinky cheese, but if you are an outdoorsy type, there are also plenty of adventures to be had, and the GR20 trail is certainly for hardcore adventurers because this is widely considered by those in the know as the toughest long distance trail in Europe. It traverses the gorgeous island of Corsica from north to south with a variation in height of about 10,000 metres, which can be walked in 15 days.

65. Wave a Rainbow Flag at Paris Gay Pride

France is a place where LGBT people can be themselves, and the ultimate party for gay people in France has to be the annual Paris Gay Pride event, which is hosted each year on the last weekend of June. There are many parties that you can attend throughout the Gay Pride festival, and the whole thing culminates in an awesome street party, and each year around 800,000 people take to the streets to see it.

(www.gaypride.fr)

66. Discover the Traboules, Renaissance Passageways, of Lyon

Lyon is the kind of the city that bears endless exploration. One of the parts of hidden Lyon that is totally fascinating are the traboules, or hidden passageways, that weave through the old quarter of the city. These secret alleyways date back to the Renaissance period when silk workers used them to get their beautiful cloth and garments to and from the market unblemished. Many of these are open in the morning time beneath private apartments, so do get exploring.

67. Catch Your Reflection in the Hall of Mirrors at Versailles

The Palace of Versailles is certainly one of best examples of magnificent royal palaces to be found anywhere in the world. It's totally possible to spend multiple days there exploring everything, but our highlight is always the famous Hall of Mirrors, the central gallery of the palace. This gallery is famous for its seventeen arches that are mirror clad and reflect the seventeen windows that overlook the gardens. It never fails to make us feel as though we have a hell of a lot of interior design work to get done in our own homes. *(Domaine National de Versailles, Place d'Armes Versailles; www.chateauversailles.fr/decouvrir/domaine/chateau/galerie-glaces)*

68. Watch Traditional Cabaret at the Moulin Rouge

When it comes to cabaret shows, there is truly nowhere more iconic than the Moulin Rouge, located in the Montmartre area on the outskirts of Paris. Unfortunately, the original building burned down in 1915, but it was rebuilt in 1921, and you can still catch cabaret performances there today. The Moulin Rouge is most famous for being the place where the can-can dance originated, created as a seductive dance by the courtesans who would perform there.

(82 Boulevard de Clichy, Paris; www.moulinrouge.fr)

69. Eat Socca on the Streets of Nice

French food is more than cream sauces and great cuts of meat. In fact, we think that some of the "peasant food" you can find around the country is the most delicious. When you are in Nice, you absolutely have to try socca. This dish, which is a chickpea based pancake, dates all the way back to the 19th century. This is the kind of hearty snack that fishermen, dockers, and workers would eat to fill themselves up. It's best eaten hot from the oven.

70. Have a Vintage Shopping Adventure in Paris

Paris is a city famous for its famous fancy boutiques and for hosting a local population with an absolutely incredible sense of their own personal style. But if you are shopping on a budget and you want to veer away from Parisian head-to-toe black, there are some alternative spots where you can shop for an outfit in the city. Goldymama is a much loved vintage clothing store with items that date right back to the 1920s.

(14 Rue du Surmelin, 75020 Paris; www.goldymama.com)

71. Take in a Show at Toulon Opera

Is Paris the centre of culture in France? Well, yes, but this is not to say that you can't find other magnificent spots around the country to take in incredible concerts and walk around galleries. Toulon is a city that is all too often overlooked but the Toulon Opera is the second largest opera house in the country, and watching a show there is a totally unforgettable experience. The house seats 1797 people, and we actually love the highest seats for the view of the whole theatre they provide.

(Boulevard de Strasbourg, 83000 Toulon; www.operadetoulon.fr)

72. Take in the Beauty of Jardin Botanique du Montet

France is a country that is completely committed to the arts, and you can't help but notice this whenever you enter a French gallery. But this commitment to aesthetics goes beyond fine art, and the French also treat their gardens exactly as though they are gorgeous paintings. This is very much apparent at the Jardin Botanique du Montet. On the outskirts of the Nancy area, these gardens have over 12,000 planets from various different continents. We specially love the greenhouses with giant waterlilies.

(www.jardinbotaniquedenancy.eu/jardin-j-m-pelt)

73. Start Your Day With a Coffee From Ten Belles

If you can't get your day started without a strong cup of coffee, have no fear because France is a nation of coffee enthusiasts, and most local people wouldn't dream of starting the day without a hit of caffeine either. Located in a trendy area and with limited seating, you'll be very lucky to snatch a place to sit and enjoy your coffee at Ten Belles, but even if you can only manage a cup to-go it's still worth going here for the friendly service, incredible sausage rolls that are made in-house, and of course, the exceptional quality of the coffee.

(10 Rue de la Grange aux Belles, 75010 Paris;
www.tenbelles.com)

74. Have a Rock Climbing Adventure at Verdon Gorge

If you have a wild, adventurous spirit, you might overlook France as somewhere just to eat pastries and go to the opera, but we promise you there are enough outdoor adventures to satisfy even the most adventurous of travellers. One place that's particularly special is Verdon Gorge, the deepest gorge in France, and one of the natural wonders of Provence. What's more, this is one of Europe's prime climbing destinations, with steep cliffs, routes that are well bolted, and views that are stunning to say the least.

(www.lesgorgesduverdon.fr/en)

75. Have a Decadent Cocktail Night at Fred's in Nice

When you're on holiday, it's time to to put your stresses behind you and to allow yourself to be more than a little bit decadent. Of course, there are incredible cocktail bars located all over the country, and we are particularly fond of an establishment called Fred's in the charming seaside city of Nice. Its cellar of around 200 different spirits means that this is a temple dedicated to cocktails, and a place where you can mingle with the hip and stylish of the city.

(9 Rue Antoine Gautier, 06000 Nice)

76. Get to Grips With Lyon's History at the Gallo-Roman Museum

It is easy to think of French history beginning in the Renaissance period when France was leading the way when it came to art, engineering, architecture, and many other fields, but there is also a Gallo-Roman ancient history in France that is best explored at the Gallo-Roman Museum in Lyon. In fact, the exhibitions start way back with the Neanderthals, the first humanoids that came from this region. This is definitely one for history buffs.

(17 Rue Cleberg, 69005 Lyon; www.museegalloromain.grandlyon.com)

77. Go Underground and Explore the Catacombs of Paris

From the eighteenth to the mid nineteenth centuries, many graveyards in and around Paris were closed for public health reasons, and the remains of around six million people were transported below the streets to what's now known as the Catacombs of Paris. These passageways can actually be visited by those interested in the city's grislier side, and we think that they're a fantastic counterpoint to the glamour and glitz of Paris as it is most commonly known and experienced.

(1 Avenue du Colonel Henri Rol-Tanguy, 75014 Paris; www.catacombes.paris.fr)

78. Explore the Loire Valley on Horseback

Although it's just a short ride away from Paris, the Loire Valley feels like a totally different world. Trade in the busy streets for greenery, quaint villages, and wonderful vineyards, and you have the Loire Valley, a beloved place among the French and international tourists alike. But if you'd like to explore the valley in a slightly more unique way, we think that on horseback is definitely the way to go. There are numerous companies that can take you from castle to castle on horseback, as you breathe in the fresh air and take in the vistas.

79. Learn How to Surf at Biarritz

It's true that France is famous for some wonderful Mediterranean beaches, but it is rarely thought of as a surfing destination. But, of course, France is a country that has it all, and if you would like to ride the waves of the Med, the coastal town of Biarritz is the place to be. Biarritz is also very unique because it's only 22km away from Spain and has that special feel of the Basque Country. There are numerous surf schools that can cater to total beginners, so simply take your pick.

80. Eat the Best Éclair of Your Life at Stohrer

One of the quintessential French sweet treats is a classic éclair, and while there are plenty of places where you can indulge in these delicious pillows of pastry, cream, and sugar, we think there is nowhere quite as magical as Stohrer in Paris. What makes this place extra special is its history – it's the oldest pastry shop in the city dating back to 1725. The crowds keep flocking through the bakery doors for the classic eclairs, and we can hardly blame them.

(51 Rue Montorgueil, Paris; http://stohrer.fr/?lang=en)

81. Celebrate African Culture in Cajarc

You probably didn't go all the way to France to learn about African cultures, but in our increasingly globalised world, it is a huge privilege to be able to explore international cultures in different places right around the world. Cajarc is a tiny little village by the River Lot where the locals like to fish for giant carp, but for one weekend in July, it comes alive with the sounds of African music and the smells of African food. We can't recommend it highly enough.

(www.africajarc.com)

82. Tour a Classic Bordeaux Vineyard, Chateau Pape Clement

If you're a wine lover, you are going to feel absolutely spoiled rotten on your trip to France, and of course, a trip to Bordeaux is an absolute must. There are numerous vineyards here, and the Cheatau Pape Clement might be the most special of them all. Planted in 1300, this is the oldest vineyard in the entire region, and you can still visit for short wine tastings, or for longer visits that allow you to stay on the premises and really soak up the incredible local wine culture.

(www.bernard-magrez.com/en/wines/chateau-pape-clement)

83. Ride a Carousel of Extinct and Endangered Animals

The Jardin des Plantes in Paris is a series of botanical gardens where it's lovely to hang out and take in some fresh air on a summer's day. But we often visit this garden for more than just the beautiful plants and serene atmosphere. Hidden away, you can find something called Dodo Manege, a funfair carousel that gives kids the opportunity to ride extinct animals such as the dodo, the horned turtle, and the barbary lion.

(57 Rue Cuvier, 75005 Paris)

84. Pay a Visit to the Graindorge Cheese Factory

Love cheese? Err, of course you do, and we're sure that's one of the major reasons why you are choosing to visit France. For us, a trip locked inside a cheesemonger would be more than satisfactory, and that's why it's our pleasure to recommend the Graindorge Cheese Factory. This dairy has been in operation since 1910, and specialises in the production of a few cheese like Camembert de Normandie and Livarot. The ideas and ingredients are simple; the results are fabulous.

(42 Rue Gén Leclerc, 14140 Livarot; www.graindorge.fr/en)

85. Party at an Electronic Music Festival, Nuits Sonores

For banging electronic music festivals, France not might be an obvious destination, but Nuits Sonores is an electronic festival that you truly will not want to miss if you love nothing more than to dance into the early hours. Hosted each May in Lyon, this festival is the place to party for serious dance music lovers. It attracts incredible DJ talent from the likes of The Chemical Brothers and Nina Kravitz. *(www.nuits-sonores.com/en)*

86. Try a Traditional Dessert of Brittany, Far Breton

When we are in Brittany, we choose to sidestep the dainty French macarons and eclairs, as a delightful as they are, for something far more robust and comforting: Far Breton. This is a stodgy dessert that is native to this part of France, and it's a simple but totally delicious treat. This is basically a stodgy flan that is filled with juicy prunes and a splash of Armagnac to make it something especially decadent.

87. Explore an 11ᵗʰ Century Abbey, Abbey of Saint-Victor

Marseilles is often thought of as a student city, and indeed, it is a really fantastic place to party, but this is not to say that there are no historic attractions to be explored in the coastal city, and one of our favourite buildings is the Abbey of Saint-Victor, which date back to the 11ᵗʰ century. While the abbey was stripped of many of its treasures in the 18ᵗʰ century, it is still used as a place of worship today.

(Place Saint-Victor, 13007 Marseille; www.saintvictor.net/?lang=en)

88. Spend a Day as a Fisherman at Haliotika

It is no secret that you can eat plates and plates of scrumptious seafood while you are in France, but have you ever thought more deeply about how the fish gets to your plate? You have exactly that opportunity at Haliotika, a fishing based attraction on the coast. Inside, you'll learn about the lives of local fishermen, fishing techniques, and you can even attend a fish auction. And if you are a keen fisherman yourself, you also have the chance to take to the seas for a day.

(Terrasse Panoramique, Le port - BP 18, 29730 Guilvinec; www.haliotika.com)

89. Stroll the Aisles of the National Museum of Modern Art

There is no doubt that Paris is an arts city through and through, but Paris is more famous for showcasing Renaissance artworks than for being a hub of contemporary creativity. But if you fancy checking out France's modern art scene, you can't go far wrong with a visit to the National Museum of Modern Art in Paris. The collection is comprehensive to say the least, with artworks by Man Ray, Max Ernst, Yves Klein, and many other famous names besides.

(11 Avenue du Président Wilson, Paris; www.mam.paris.fr/en)

90. Listen to the Cheep Cheeps of the Paris Bird Market

Europe has a wonderful market culture, and France is certainly no exception to that rule. Of course, there are so many markets where you can buy local cheese and plump olives, but if you fancy visiting a market with a difference, we would love to recommend the

Paris Bird Market, which takes over the centre of the city every Sunday. You can hear the cheeping of the birds for miles around, and strolling the aisles of the market certainly does add colour to the city streets.

(Place Louis Lépine, 75001 Paris)

91. Enjoy the Quietude of Porquerolles Island

Have you heard of the Porquerolles island before? Probably not as this island is still very much undiscovered. We can't quite fathom why because this place is seriously gorgeous, and if you want to discover the wild beauty of France, we think that it's a must visit island. The island lies just south of St Tropez, with rugged cliffs to the south and almost always empty beaches on the north side of the island.

92. Enjoy Cocktails With a View at Le Perchoir Marais

Paris is a stunning city, but there are more luxurious ways to take in the city than by walking the city streets. When our feet are tired from walking from museum to museum, we like to perch ourselves on a rooftop bar and watch city life pass us by with a cocktail in hand. For our money, Le Perchoir Marais is the ultimate spot for this. And if cocktails and a view isn't decadent enough, they also serve up yummy lobster sandwiches.

(33 Rue de la Verrerie, 75004 Paris; www.leperchoir.tv)

93. Look at France's Oldest Wall Painting in Sainte Chapelle

Paris has no shortage of stunning historic buildings, and Sainte Chapelle is certainly one of the most beautiful of the lot. The Gothic style makes this chapel stand out from the crowd, but it's what's inside the church that is seriously impressive. For starters, it houses one of the most impressive collections of 13th century stained glass found anywhere in the world. And beyond that, it has France's oldest wall painting, a depiction of The Annunciation.

(8 Boulevard du Palais, 75001 Paris; www.sainte-chapelle.fr)

94. Cross the Tallest Bridge in the World, the Millau Viaduct

France has no shortage of impressive structures, but look beyond the churches and castles, and there are more contemporary feats to be explored. Take the Millau Viaduct, for example, which is a bridge that spans the length of the gorge valley of the River Tarn. This bridge isn't just something pretty to look at – it's the highest bridge in the world, with a height of 343 metres. We think it's well worth renting a car and motoring across.

(Grands Causses Natural Regional Park, Viaduc de Millau, 12400 Millau)

95. Eat the World's Best Bouillabaisse at Chez Fonfon, Marseille

While it's true that a lot of French food can be quite heavy, you shouldn't forget that France also has a great deal of beautiful coastline, and this means that the country also does fish and seafood dishes very well indeed. One of the classic seafood dishes from the Provence region is bouillabaisse, which is a stew containing red rascasse, sea robin, conger, and shellfish like sea urchins, crab, and mussels. Our favourite spot for a steaming hot bowl of the good stuff is Chez Fonfon in Marseilles.

(140 Rue du Vallon des Auffes, 13007 Marseille; www.chez-fonfon.com)

96. Take in a View of the Black Forest From Strasbourg Cathedral

Strasbourg is the capital of the Grand Est region, and because of its proximity to Germany it has a very different feel to some of the other cities in the country. We think that this is all the more reason to pay a visit, and once you set your eyes on Strasbourg Cathedral we don't think that you'll regret making the trip eastwards. This was the tallest cathedral in the world for almost 200 years, and you can climb to the cathedral platform, where you'll have an astounding view of the Black Forest in Germany.

(Place de la Cathédrale, 67000 Strasbourg; www.cathedrale-strasbourg.fr)

97. Listen to Some Smooth Sounds at Nice Jazz Festival

If you like the idea of attending a summer festival in France, but you are not so taken by electronic music or big rock acts, the Nice Jazz Festival might be something that it is more up your alley. We especially love the location of the festival, which is hosted is some very charming gardens between Place Massena and the beach. The festival can accommodate 6000 jazz lovers, and acts that have performed in the past include Ella Fitzgerald and Miles Davis.

(www.nicejazzfestival.fr/en)

98. Purchase a Luxurious Box of Chocolates at La Maison du Chocolat

In this world there are two types of people. Those who recognise that chocolate is the food of the Gods, and very silly people indeed. You need to treat yourself with at least one box of chocolates while you're in France, and in our opinion, there is absolutely no better place to do so than at La Maison du Chocolat in Paris. With a mix of classic and inventive flavours, it's always our go-to spot when we need a treat.

(Carrousel du Louvre, 99 Rue de Rivoli, 75001 Paris; www.lamaisonduchocolat.fr/)

99. Create Your Own Blend of Cognac

There is plenty of decadence that comes from France: the wine, the eclairs, the macarons. But when we are feeling especially decadent, our first port of call is always cognac, a brandy from the town of Cognac made from distilled grapes. Camus is a family owned Cognac brand in the town, and it's well worth visiting their distillery. Not only can you taste some of the good stuff, but you can actually create your very own blend of Cognac to take home with you.

(www.camus.fr/fr)

100. Explore 70 Rooms of Art at Musee des Beaux Arts in Lyon

While Paris is certainly a wonderful city to visit if you wish to visit art museums, it doesn't have a monopoly on this aspect of French culture, and we'd also recommend a trip to the Musee des Beaux Arts in Lyon if you are the artsy type. Inside, you will find a huge range of things from Egyptian Antiquities and right up to Modern Art. As you might expect, it's particularly great for showcasing French works of art, including artists like Cezanne, Manet, and Renoir.

(20 Place des Terreaux, 69001 Lyon; www.mba-lyon.fr/mba/sections/languages/welcome)

101. Camp Under the Stars Around Lake Annecy

France is most certainly an exciting country, where there is plenty to do, see, and eat, but when we just want to relax, unwind, and let the weight of the world fall from our shoulders, we always choose to visit Lake Annecy. There's plenty to enjoy here, from swimming in the crystal clear waters to taking scenic bike rides. What's more, there are a couple of camping grounds set around the lake, so you can sleep under the stars and truly immerse yourself in the French landscape.

Before You Go...

Thanks for reading **101 Coolest Things to Do in France.** We hope that it makes your trip a memorable one!

Keep your eyes peeled on www.101coolestthings.com, and have a wonderful time in France.

Team 101 Coolest Things

Made in the USA
San Bernardino, CA
22 November 2017